Acknowledgements

Thank you to the athletes for sharing their stories.

Thank you to Jamie Baulch and Hannah Hore at Definitive Sports Management; Gayle Howells at Seren PR; and Jane Thomas and Sarah Mogford at Sport Wales for their help.

Foreword

For our Welsh sportsmen and sportswomen the London 2012 Olympics will be the high point of a long and difficult journey. As we follow them in their quest to take on the world's best athletes, we will marvel at their skills and competitive spirit, developed over many years of dedication and commitment. Just as it did for me, their Olympic dream began with an inspiration which might have come from their mum or dad, an enthusiastic school teacher, local club coach or by watching their heroes on television and wanting to equal their great feats.

For me, it was a chance meeting with Ron Pickering, the National Athletics coach for Wales, which fired my desire to compete in the Olympics. His great ability to guide me as a young athlete, motivate and inspire me to higher levels of training, and support me when things went wrong, played a huge role in helping me to win the gold medal for the long jump at the Tokyo Olympic Games.

In sport, as in life, there are setbacks and

hurdles to overcome. Injuries, illness, loss of form and confidence all play their part. The challenge is to keep a clear focus on the goals and stay motivated to achieve them.

In modern sport no one can make the grade by working alone. Champions come from teamwork – the support people such as the coach, trainer, sport scientist and medical staff. No stone is left unturned in the pursuit of your dream.

There are many people with natural ability but who lack the commitment needed to spend hours every day honing their skills and fitness levels. The Welsh athletes who will represent us in London 2012 will have paid this price and made the necessary sacrifices. Their reward will be to take part in the greatest sporting event on earth, the Olympic Games. They will join an elite club of people who have reached the top of their sport. We in Wales will follow their progress over the coming months and feel very proud when we watch them take on the best in the world.

Good luck.

Lynn Davies CBE, President UK Athletics, Olympic gold medallist Tokyo 1964

David 'Dai' Greene

Hurdler

Technique, tenacity and talent ... those are the qualities that sum up Dai Greene. A passionate athlete and a passionate Welshman, his focus and determination have taken him to the top. He deserves to succeed. Greene for go! Da iawn, Dai!

Colin Jackson CBE, 1993 and 1999 World Champion 110 metres hurdles

I was at my happiest in school when I was playing sport. I did enjoy my other studies but sport was what I wanted to do. My earliest success was winning the local cross-country race in Llanelli at the age of seven. I only lived five minutes away from school and I ran home shouting, 'I won! I won!' clutching my medal proudly to show my parents, who hadn't expected me to win at all. David Tanner was my headmaster at Penygaer Junior school in Llanelli and he took a keen interest in me and still follows me in competitions now. He could see I had a talent and the desire to do well, and he always challenged me in a good and competitive way and this helped and influenced me as a youngster.

To be fair, all of the teachers knew I loved taking part in sport and noticed early on that I was a good all-rounder. I wanted to be involved in every sport that was open to me. The teachers were very supportive and often stayed behind after school to help with our sporting activities to ensure we were really well prepared when we had competitions. Again, when I went to secondary school, Coedcae in Llanelli, my teachers Mike Walters and Nick Murphy stayed behind after school to work with me, which is a sacrifice they didn't have to make and which I very much appreciate now. My parents didn't shower me with compliments about my sporting successes, but took me wherever I wanted to compete without complaining. They never pushed me into anything, the choice was mine. But I was always keen to get involved and they were keen to help me. They just wanted me to be happy and I think that is a great attitude. It made sport fun and not a chore. As a child you don't think about all that your parents do for you but, looking back on it, they drove miles to a training venue, then hung around waiting for me for several hours and then drove me back. It can't have been much fun for them!

I signed with Swansea City football club at an early age and I enjoyed playing for them for a number of years. Then, sadly, I had one season where I lost confidence. I stopped enjoying football and started to question why I was doing it. My parents were supportive of me and let me join a smaller local team so that I could begin enjoying myself again. They just wanted to see me happy and I decided to turn down the contract in Swansea because it wasn't for me at that time. I loved football but I needed a less forceful approach to get the best out of me. I lacked confidence and I didn't react well to being shouted at. It didn't bring out the best in me. Now I am older I can deal with a strong approach but then I wasn't able to handle it and I performed poorly because of it. It was a vicious circle because the more upset I got, the worse I played and so the best thing was for me to leave. It took me a number of years to get my confidence back but when I did the proof was my success.

Growing up I idolised Ryan Giggs. He played on the left wing and I was naturally right footed, so

I taught myself at a very early age to play with my left foot. I practised in the garden dribbling around cricket wickets and I picked it up very quickly and easily. People didn't know which foot I naturally used as I could kick with both feet equally well. It became second nature for me to use both as I had such good control. Later, it really helped when it came to hurdling, as I could use both legs equally well and had excellent coordination. I didn't know then just how much a favour I was doing myself by practising those soccer skills. They were to be a huge help in my later athletics career!

I had always loved athletics in school in the summer months, so when I left football I decided to use the time to train more in my new-found sport, hurdling. I'd train twice a week but I'd also be out at the weekends having a few drinks with my mates, so I was never really that good at competitions as I wasn't giving a hundred per cent effort. At the age of seventeen I was diagnosed with epilepsy, a condition which my brother also has. I suffered a few seizures but I decided that if I changed my lifestyle and concentrated on my sports, then epilepsy was not going to stop me doing anything. I know my trigger points and I am lucky because my condition is not severe.

When I went to university, at the University of Wales Institute, Cardiff (UWIC), I met people who were as serious about training as I had been when I played football, and they encouraged me to join them in a group that trained every day. I started doing weights with them and as soon as I got involved, I never looked back. All the old desire to do well returned. I hadn't really known what I wanted to do with my life when I went to university. I hadn't wanted to study anything in particular. But when I got there, I rediscovered athletics and remembered how much I loved training. Also, because I had enjoyed a good social life earlier, partying was out of my system. I was able to make the most of college and was motivated by having people around me who wanted to get the most out of their sport and out of their lives. I also met my girlfriend, Sian, at UWIC as she was in the same training group as me.

I studied Sport and Leisure Management and my coach there was Darrell Maynard. I worked with Darrell from 2004 to 2008 and I'm still very close to him. Our relationship may be coach and athlete but I'm always welcome at his house for Sunday lunch with his family, and he is a very important part of my career. He helped me by

5

example. He showed me how fit he was – as a forty-year-old man he trained with the group and often put us to shame! He brought enjoyment and energy to the track every day. He helped me enjoy athletics and acted like a father figure to me when I lived away from home. He helped to finish off and mould me into the person I am today. He was ex-army so he didn't take any nonsense in training, and he commanded respect from us all. He put an ethos of hard work into our training group and that's something that's stuck with me. If I had been with a different coach for those three years at university, I would never have been as successful as I am now. I have a great deal to thank him for.

Within a year of training with Darrell, I was selected for the European Juniors and I became European Junior silver medallist in 2005 and European Under-23 champion in 2007. But 2008 was tough. I was injured that year and I could only watch the competitions on television. It was a strange experience for me. I enjoyed watching the Beijing Olympics but of course I really wanted to have been there. Some people might have thought that I had reached my limit but I was positive and knew I would come back stronger than ever. I used the year to motivate myself, and told myself that the setbacks would make me better, and more determined to be a winner. Not going to the Beijing Olympics turned out to be a great positive. It gave me the hunger to train harder and to make myself mentally stronger so that, whatever came my way, I could deal with it. The improvement came quickly in the next year, 2009, when I became a World Championship finalist. Very quickly I went from being just a good promising youngster to being one of the best in the world. It was a great experience for me.

I started 2010 well by winning the European Championships in Barcelona, where I was the favourite. I ran a personal best in the final, with my parents and my girlfriend watching, and I was very close to tears as I took my victory lap. Seeing my parents after the race also made me realise how much my success meant to them. The win gave me a huge boost of confidence. However, leading up to my next challenge, the Commonwealth Games in Delhi, I was really ill and at one point I wasn't even sure that I would make the start line. The Commonwealth Games are so important for the nations taking part and it seemed like everyone in Wales knew I was there! I went into the race as a main medal contender and really felt the pressure of expectation. People kept telling me to be the first Welsh gold medallist on the team! I remember being in the call room beforehand, preparing to go out to race, but all I remember about the event is being on the track in the start position and then the last few hurdles. Winning for Wales was a great moment, as was knowing how much it meant to the team to see the Welsh dragon flying for us. Being in Delhi was special for me, because I was rooming with my Welsh teammates, whom I didn't get to see very often as I lived and outside Wales. We all enjoyed ourselves and our room in the team village felt like being in Cardiff! Gareth Warburton, James Thie, Christian Malcolm, and Joe Thomas joined me in playing computer games and we all relaxed together before the races. Colin Jackson gave us huge support from the commentary box and it was good to see how much it meant for everyone back home.

For me, it's very important to love what you're doing. I believe that you won't be successful unless you really enjoy what you're doing and you give it your all. Obviously, I train very hard, but I actively enjoy the challenge of the months of training, and the commitment I have to give, to achieve my goals. I love the journey of getting to the start line. I love coming in every day to work really hard and I've always been like that. I never wanted to leave the pitch until we were kicked off and it's the same for me when I train for athletics competitions around the world. I don't look at the other guys on the start line in a race. I'm there to win. If I'm struggling to finish in a training session then I imagine my opponents winning, and that's enough motivation for me to get on with things. I respect my competitors but I'm not fazed by titles. It just makes the challenge greater, and I rise to a challenge. My heroes are the ones who are really dedicated to what they do. Ryan Giggs worked hard and adapted the way he plays to fit the modern game. Colin Jackson was amazing because his effort and dedication were renowned in the sport.

After my coach, Benke Blomkvist, returned to Sweden, I left Cardiff and relocated to train at the University of Bath under Malcolm Arnold. He is a fantastic motivator and the facilities at Bath are second to none. It's got a lovely outdoor track, an indoor straight which is ideal for winter training, great grounds to go running in and the gym is superb. Everything is geared towards success and winning. When you finish a training session, you go and have food in the canteen and are surrounded by other top class athletes from other sports. I am very happy there.

I have a hunger to be the best and, for me, becoming a better athlete and becoming a better person go hand in hand. I challenge myself and push myself because I'm never content with minimum effort. I always want that little bit more. When you achieve success it's a great feeling because you've trained all those months for one night, one race. My coach Malcolm Arnold, like Darrell, believes that hard work brings results. He is highly respected and in the past worked with John Akii Bua and Colin Jackson. For him there is no magic formula, just good old-fashioned hard work. He instils a tough mental attitude in his athletes and knows how to bring out the best in us all. Ours is a great partnership and I admire his honesty and the fact that he challenges me.

There is no question that Malcolm prepared me well for the World Championships in Daegu. I had shown consistently good form throughout the season and felt calm and relaxed and ready to race. Despite two false starts, I kept my composure and confidence, and came home in 48.26 seconds, ahead of Javier Culson and L. J.

van Zyl, to win the gold medal and join a very select band of Welsh World Championship medallists.

I'm now Commonwealth Champion, European Champion and World Champion. Next is 2012 with a home Olympics. I couldn't ask for more in my career. I hope it inspires many others to work towards their own dreams.

Nathan Stephens

JAVELIN AND DISCUS

Nathan is one of the most inspirational young athletes I have ever met. His dedication to his sport is matched by his positive outlook on life and his total belief he can achieve his goals. He is a great role model to us all and a credit to Welsh sport. Good luck, Nathan, in London 2012. You can win gold!'

Lynn Davies CBE, President UK Athletics, Olympic gold medallist 1964

Rugby and football were my passions when I was a child and I used to follow my brother Andrew around, imagining we were playing for Wales. I was a very good defender and goalkeeper in football and my grandad wanted me to be grow up to be a great Welsh prop. But all that changed on my ninth birthday, when I was run over by a train while playing on the track. We loved to go and play alongside the moving trains, as kids then did. But that day was different. We ran next to a slow freight train, tapping it, and I decided to try to jump on one of the ladders. I don't remember exactly what happened next, but somehow my foot slipped and I was dragged under. My friend Ricky dragged me off the track and my brother and my cousin Josh ran to get help. Luckily, they met a woman who gave me drinks to keep me hydrated as I drifted in and out of consciousness. I remember waking up, looking down and seeing one leg had gone, and that the other was in a very bad way. I also remember seeing the fire brigade arrive and them cutting off my new Manchester United shirt, which I wasn't very happy about. As my dad had just started his night shift, it was my grandad, George, who got there to lift me into the ambulance. I remember feeling excited about being taken in a helicopter, an air ambulance, on my birthday. I've never been able to ask my friends what they saw or how they felt that day.

In hospital, I couldn't sit up at all because of the scarring. I had lost both my legs and needed a mechanical bed to raise me up and down. I soon became fed up with machines having to help me but I was told it would take a long time to do without them. I wasn't going to accept this and after a couple of weeks I forced myself, despite the pain, and gritted my teeth and managed to sit up! My mum and I were in tears when she saw what I had managed and we knew nothing could stop me now. I was determined. I just knew I wasn't going to be sitting in a hospital bed for the rest of my life, or in a wheelchair doing nothing. I saw how others in hospital refused to be beaten and I wanted that for me.

The first sport I took up was sledge hockey, after speaking to Aaron Rees who was playing at the time. He asked me if I had thought about sport. I hadn't imagined what sport I could do now. He said, 'Sledge hockey! We sit down on the ice – it's great! It's fast, it's fun and it's full contact!' My eyes lit up, but as I said yes, my mum's face said no. She wanted time to think, to protect me against any future disappointments and pain, but just the idea gave me the push to get out of hospital and get better, so that I could return to school and back to my friends. My nurse was the mum of Jonathan Humphreys, the Cardiff and Wales rugby player, and she brought me a pair of his socks and shorts and that spurred me on, knowing that people wanted to help me. My school friends and teachers were fantastic. They told me not to let anything get in my way and said that they would help me with whatever I tried. They never put up any barriers and my parents were the same. They said, 'Try whatever and we'll support you, no matter what.' Back in school, I started to think about what I could do so that I could play with my friends again. I sat in goal in football games and in rugby I would sit in the middle of the field, wait for the players to come towards me and then jump on them. They didn't make the same mistake twice! I knew school was there to help me to reach my potential. But outside of school was different. For a while I was nervous about going out, and friends had to come and see me in my bedroom. I wasn't sure how people would react to me. But in the end I decided I would face the world and whatever people had to say to me. The day I decided to go out was like being released from a kind of prison, the day when normality returned.

The sledge hockey team reinforced that feeling. I had never seen so many disabilities and there was no chance to be shy as everyone insulted each other with a smile. It was also good for my parents and my brother to see how I coped. When I got onto the ice rink for the first time I was in a giant sled too big for me, with kit that didn't fit, and my head was too small for any of the helmets. But I came off the ice beaming. The coach was worried that I was too small and too young to play, and my mother was terrified for me, but was determined I should do what made me happy and the coach backed down. The hours were hard as the only ice time we could get was about eleven o'clock at night for two hours so I would get home really late and then had to get up early for school the next day. My mum made it clear that school was a priority and if I didn't wake up on time in the mornings, I wouldn't be playing. I never missed a morning in school and, despite playing with seniors and being the smallest on the ice, I didn't miss a challenge. I got myself ready to play and counted my bruises and scars. This was what I wanted to do. In my first competitive game, I cried because I was young, and the other team realised they could rattle me and wind me up, but I learnt to deal with the names they called me and soon understood that it was because they knew I was quick and could be good that they tried to put me off my game. There were times when I found it hard and wanted to quit but I always came back. I told myself that I would just take it out on them on the ice when I got bigger and stronger. In my first international competition I was teased for my baby face, as usual. My pads were too big for me and rode up and down, and as I defended one of the Swedish team hit me in the ribs with the puck and I went down like a sack of spuds, crying and rolling on the ice. My dad dragged me off to hospital thinking that I had broken a rib but I was only bruised. And I had stopped them scoring! Sledge hockey toughened me up physically and mentally. The banter between teammates made me strong against bullying outside and I was able to look after myself. They would say to me, 'Nathan, you know it's only words. We don't mean it. We just like to wind you up before you get on the ice.' I learnt quickly that people would always find ways to get at you and I had to learn to deal with it. Even now, I miss the team banter. It made me able to face whatever life threw at me.

Moving from Mynydd Cynffig to my secondary school, Ynysawdre, I had to leave my friends. I couldn't join them at the local school because I needed wheelchair access and Ynysawdre was the only school locally with a disability unit. I didn't know anybody there and I sat in the corner hoping that someone would come and talk to me because I was quite shy. But in the end I started to talk to people and became part of the group. I got on with everyone, talking about the rock music I loved and my sport.

Again, my headteacher, Mr Woodwards, and my PE teacher, Mr Moore, came to the rescue. They let me try all sports in mainstream PE because I didn't want to be classed as different or be separated from the others. Whatever they were doing in PE I said, 'That's OK, I'll adapt and I'll do something.' I got involved with rugby, I played cricket for the school as wicketkeeper and bowler, and enjoyed swimming as part of my physiotherapy. I'd always loved swimming and the pool was somewhere I could almost match my fellow pupils. One of my teachers knew David Roberts and she got him to come to see me and show me his Olympic medal, and straight away I knew I wanted one of those around my neck. I didn't care in which sport – I just wanted to win one! David became a great mentor to me and took me to Caerphilly Dragons. I began swimming with him every week while still playing hockey, and before long I competed for Wales in breaststroke and in the individual medley. I could never get far in front crawl, though, as David, the great Paralympic champion, was still competing. He was phenomenal in the pool and a huge inspiration to everyone who watched him swim.

At the Newport Rotary Games, I was spotted by Anthony Hughes (now my coach) who encouraged me to try athletics. It wasn't something we did in school and I had always associated athletics with track events and had never thought of field events. He got me interested in javelin, shot and discus. I had a good arm and strong shoulders from playing cricket in school and he made me practise throwing a ball against the wall. He said that my technique was useless but that I had strength. For eighteen months he made me throw rubber rings, balls and other dog toys to improve my technique. A year later I competed in the British Junior Championships in Blackpool and came back with three gold medals in shot-put, javelin and discus! This then qualified me for the Senior Championships in Birmingham, and I returned from that with two golds and a silver, and broke the British Senior record!

I had to make a decision about which sport to focus on because I was now doing three – hockey, swimming and athletics. I needed to choose. I knew that there were others better than me in swimming, so that would be one to drop. And I was told by my athletics coach that I could be the best thrower Britain had ever produced, so I was determined to stick with that. But then the GB Sledge Hockey coach rang me to ask me to train with the squad. He told me that I was the best sledge hockey player in Britain for my age and I was thrilled with that. The youngest and the best sounded good to me – but what a choice to have to make!

My parents made sure my school-work didn't suffer and I got twelve GCSEs, including maths which I took a year early, while also training. I took A levels and a BTEC in Sport and Exercise Science to help me with my training and my understanding of body mechanics. Most weekends I had to go to Hull to train, and my parents were fantastic. They would drive the five hours there and the five hours back without ever complaining. I was chosen to compete in the 2004 World Championships in Sweden and I scored the winning goal which meant the team qualified to go on to Turin to compete in the Winter Paralympics there. Throughout all of this my parents were there on side, ensuring I could do what I loved. Without them I would never have achieved what I have done and their love and support is what has made me the athlete I am today.

When I was chosen for Great Britain to compete in the 2004 Paralympics in Turin I attended the opening ceremony proudly in my first GB kit. I was seventeen years old. We were all nervous but being in such a strong team environment helped calm us all down. We knew we were in it together and we all felt the same way. I was the youngest, and so proud to be there. I absolutely loved it. We were beaten by the Canadian and American teams but I refused to stop smiling. Those teams trained together full-time while we trained once a month, and just to be able to compete against the best in the world was amazing. But we were determined not to finish last and got to sudden death in the last quarter. I was playing defence and suddenly thought I had to go for it. I went straight down the middle in front of the net and shouted across. I was passed the puck, shut my eyes and hit it. I didn't want to know what had happened and, without looking, went to skate off. I turned around to see the whole team ploughing towards me – I had scored! Everyone piled on top of me to celebrate that we had won a game and wouldn't finish last. And later, even with my parents there, I still managed to sneak away with the Swedish team and celebrate properly!

I had to make a decision with my coach about my future. He pointed out that I had to choose between continuing to play hockey and competing in athletics and being 'OK', or to concentrate solely on athletics and, in his words, becoming one of the greatest. I hated having to make the choice because sledge hockey was the sport that had got me moving again. It was close to my heart because it had restarted my life. And I had so many friends there. But athletics would give me a career, and I wanted to win medals like the one Dave Roberts had used to inspire me.

My first GB athletics competition was the European Championships in Espoo, Finland. Suddenly, after being part of a team, I was on my own, and it was scary. I was used to having a team of buddies around me and I didn't like this more individual set-up. I needed to make friends and when Kim Mimmet, Brian Aldiss, Nicky Bushell and I bonded together, it suddenly got more enjoyable. Kim taught me the importance of making the effort to talk to others and creating your own group to give yourself confidence. I had always relied on Anthony, my coach, to be there and his friendship and expertise were crucial to me. He had made me into the thrower that I was and I wanted him to be there every single time I competed. Now I had to learn to become stronger and more independent. It was good for me to have to learn to open up. I learnt to talk about my accident and use my experiences to help others. I wanted to be like my heroes had been to me. I was in awe of Dame Tanni Grey-Thompson, who mentored me, and I couldn't believe that this outstanding athlete was so down-to-earth and willing to help everyone around her. Lynn Davies, Lynn the Leap, also showed me the importance of motivating others and spending time encouraging others to achieve. Those two legends of Welsh sport were inspirational.

I've competed in two World Championships, the first at Assen, and the second at Christchurch, New Zealand, where I won a gold medal in javelin. My parents travelled across the world to proudly support me. My nana's bridesmaid, who had emigrated to New Zealand three years previously, was also there in the stands and held up a phone so that my nana could hear my live interview after winning! I've taken part in the European Championships in Espoo and two Paralympic Games but I haven't been able to compete in the Commonwealth Games, even though I was selected for the team in Melbourne, as my classification was changed and I wasn't able to take part. I've always wanted to wear the Welsh vest so I'm hoping that I'll have my chance in Glasgow in 2014. I can't wait for London in 2012 because I'm hoping that my whole family can be there. My grandad wanted me to play rugby for Wales, but he's just as proud of my athletics career, and for him to come and see me compete, cheering alongside my friends and girlfriend, would be the best thing ever for me. He couldn't get to Beijing, so didn't see me compete there.

My mum and dad understood the pressure that I felt under in Beijing and told me to just go out and enjoy it, whatever the result. The first time in the call-up room was unlike anything I had known before. I hadn't thought what it was going to be like, sitting in a little cubicle with thirteen other guys, twice my size and twice my age. I was sitting in a corner shaking like a baby at the thought of what was ahead. When I pushed out into the stadium all I could see were Chinese flags and the noise was deafening. Dotted around in the distance were GB flags and I thought, 'I'm not ready for this.' The Bird's Nest stadium wrapped around me and everything echoed as the crowds screamed their support. I remember thinking how amazing it was that I had made it to Beijing, to compete against the best in the world. It was humbling to think I might even have a chance. I finished eighth in the shot and eleventh in the discus competitions. Still to come was the javelin, the best of my events. On the night before the competition I really worked myself up and put too much pressure on myself, so much so that at midnight I rang my coach who, as ever, sorted me out by telling me to stop worrying, shut up, and go to sleep! The next day, in front of 94,000 people, I managed to get to third spot in my first Paralympics but one of my rivals was still to come and could still beat me. I couldn't watch as the Czech thrower Rostislav Pohlmann made his final attempt. I could hear my coach shouting, 'Foul throw, foul throw', but it was further than mine and I was knocked back to fourth position and out of the medals. I was twenty years old and he was forty-three. So I just said, 'I'll probably get you next time.' All I could think of after that was that London was next and I would fight hard to get the medal then.

I don't think I have done anything really special, but I've pieced my life back together again, thanks to the support and love of my family. They mean everything to me and I want to make them proud. I want something for them, for all the hard work and effort they've put in for me. Being number one is living the dream. I am a World Champion and World record holder at twenty-three years of age. I love my sport. I work hard at it and I don't ever take it for granted. I try to focus on the way forward, not looking back on what might have been. What's important to me is that I conduct myself well and compete fairly and honestly. For me it's about hard graft and hard work ... and a lot of fun along the way.

Jazmin 'Jazz' Carlin

SWIMMER

Jazz is an inspirational role model for young people, fully committed to her sport and her studies. A wonderfully warm person yet dogged and determined in the pool, she has set herself clear goals in her drive and ambition to become a successful Olympic swimmer. I wish her well.

Mark Foster, Commonwealth, European and World Championship gold medallist – swimming

In my primary school in Swindon, we had swimming races against the teachers and I won – I even beat the headmaster! It was great fun and the friendly atmosphere meant that everyone enjoyed swimming. Even at a very young age, I wanted to get everyone involved and to love it as much as I did. I always went to the pool with my dad, just enjoying myself learning the basics of swimming. Then I joined a local club and I remember that my first competition was in

Llanelli at the local pool, and it consisted of four 50-metres races finishing up with a 100 metres individual medley race. I was eighth after the 50-metre races, but ended up winning, and I got my first trophy! I've still got that trophy and I'm very proud of it! My mum and dad were there cheering me on and it has great memories for me. I was nine or ten years of age. I wasn't the best of swimmers when I was young – in fact, you could say I was a late developer but I loved racing. From the beginning, I've been a racer. I just love competing!

I went to Wootton Bassett comprehensive and I actually helped teach swimming there. It was quite hard because it was a hectic schedule: I had early morning training sessions and again in the evenings, as well as my school-work. Also, I used to get ill fairly regularly as my body was changing but I wouldn't give in. Now, looking back at it, I really don't know how I did it. It was hard fitting in school-work on top of all the swimming training but when you are younger you take things in your stride, and if you really love something you make the time and effort. I had great friends and liked school. I don't remember being tired because I was doing what I loved doing. We were given a year book when we left school and one of the categories in the book was 'The one most likely to make the Olympics' and I was nominated as that person. They knew me well! That was always my goal and, fingers crossed, I will be there!

I joined a local club in Swindon, Tiger Sharks. It was a small club with volunteer coaches. I now realise what a difference volunteers can make in sport because so many were there for me. I would not be where I am now if I hadn't had all the 'Learn to swim' lessons I did. The coaches in these sessions took time to help us develop and achieve our potential. When I was fifteen, my dad had a stroke, and since he was a young man that was really hard for us all to take. We were a close family. He was in Oxford in hospital and we lived in Swindon, so I'd go up to see him and then I'd swim in a swimming pool in Oxford with one of the coaches there. I'd try to make the best use of my time by swimming and it kept my mind off my worries about my dad. I swam in the European Junior Championships in that year and gained a bronze medal which was for my dad because he wasn't allowed to fly and so couldn't come to see me compete. Then, sadly, he had another stroke when I was sixteen and he's had various seizures since, so it's always been difficult. But we are very close as a family and they're such a great support for me, just as I'm always there for them. They always manage to make it to my competitions and it's a great inspiration to me. My dad's been a great fighter and it proves to me that I can't give up on my dreams. I have to follow his example and be the best I can for him.

I moved to Swansea at the age of sixteen and became part of the Welsh National squad. I moved to Swansea because of the retirement of my coach, Phil Millard, Head Coach of Tiger Sharks. I had been with him from the age of ten, and he was a wonderful coach and a huge inspiration to me. I'd been told by Swim Wales that they were getting a new coach in the National Pool in Swansea who was a distance specialist and who had coached the American ex-world record holder Janet Evans, and I wanted to come to train in Wales to learn from him. In Swindon, there hadn't been a great deal of training available and so moving to Swansea was a big step up for me in the right direction, and I wanted to take that opportunity.

In 2006, I was fortunate enough to represent Wales at the Commonwealth Games in Melbourne, Australia. This was a daunting experience for me. I was a young girl joining a strong team which contained the likes of David Davies, who had already got an Olympic medal. But we were all young and thanks to other members of the Welsh team we soon bonded. They took me under their wing. Wales may be one of the smaller teams but it's definitely one of the most supportive. Everyone pulls together to get the best out of each other. Jemma Lowe, a fellow competitor, who was the same age as me, shared a room with me and we became great friends and shared rooms at other competitions. I think it's important to have such friendships; they make you feel more at home when you are away on training camps or at major competitions. Although my results in Melbourne were not great, it was a terrific learning experience and with my new coach Bud McCallister in Swansea, I was determined to improve on this and look towards medals in the future.

Bud has to take most of the credit for my improvement. In the four years that I have been with him, he's got me onto the senior teams and helped me to gain medals. His nickname for me is Pitbull, which he says is because of my fighting spirit. He recognised very quickly that I like to fight and that I try my hardest in all I do, and I take the nickname as a real compliment from him. Bud is a very special coach who is always suggesting new ideas to stimulate and encourage me. I have so much respect for him as a coach and his results speak volumes. The whole team has a great relationship with him and his relaxed style of working gets the best out of us. He gives us the responsibility for working hard but, in the end, we know to do as he tells us if we want to succeed.

Having to move house to go and live in Swansea and leave my mum and dad in Swindon was hard at first. I used to go home a lot because I think it was hard for my mum and dad too. My mum said she missed the normal things, like doing my washing and ironing, that made us a family. I have aunts and uncles who live in Abergavenny and Monmouth, and it's lovely for me to know that I have family who aren't far away. We're all close and that is very important to me.

A typical training day starts very early with my alarm going off at 5.25 in the morning. I manage to have a little breakfast and then I'm in the pool between six and eight o'clock. Normally then I'll go and see the physiotherapist, and then go into the gym three times a week. After that I'll have a sleep or a rest, go back to the physiotherapist, and then go back to the pool between three and five thirty in the afternoon. A schedule like this makes family life and its support system important. You need people there for you on the phone at the end of a long day. Relaxing is crucial and what works for me is listening to music, watching films and going out with my friends – typical, really!

When it comes to racing, everything I do has to be planned down to the last detail. I need to know what time to be at the pool and to make sure that I'm not late. I follow a set routine to see the physiotherapist and start my warm-up. Then back to the physiotherapist, another quick warm-up and a word with my coach ... and I'm ready to race.

Going to the World Championships in Rome in 2009 was a buzz for me. It was my first time on the GB senior team and we got the bronze medal in the 4 × 200 metres freestyle relay. The team, Joanne Jackson, Caitlin McClatchey, Rebecca Adlington and me, also managed to set a European record. I remember walking to the side of the pool with the others and experiencing that fantastic feeling that here was everything I had worked towards. It's hard to describe how amazing it is to hear the crowd cheering and see flags waving as the teams get into position. Everyone is nervous, but excited too, and the best thing about the relay is you are there as part of a team, supporting and helping each other. This meet was really special for me. They were my first World Championships, with a great feeling of team spirit and a medal at the end! It was my chance to go out and prove myself, and I took it! We all swim against each other when we're in the individual races but come together for the relay. We're all great friends and that's definitely important. When we come together for the team we support each other one hundred per cent. For the relay we got ourselves relay pants, which we called our 'lucky pants', and they lived up to their name! We took them off as we came on to the blocks at the start but the famous pink flamingo pants were an important part of our team. We were all prepared and ready in our order of racing. We knew who was around us and the tactics to use. Preparation is crucial. I like to do my own race plan and revise it with my coach. It's important to train in the way that suits you, specially as my race plan is different from everyone else's. I tend to have a lot of back-end speed because I'm a distance swimmer and I try to use that to my advantage but still try to be competitive in the early stages. Everyone's tactics are different but what matters is that it works for you. We all pushed each other along saying, 'C'mon girls, we can do it. We're strong.' We boosted each other's confidence and deep down we all knew we were strong. What was wonderful was that we were all fighting from the heart and that is essential. Jo Jackson led off, with me as the second leg. The commentators announced that I had a bad start, which is something I know I have. For the first 100 metres, I was sixth or seventh in the race but in the second 100 metres, I came into my own and was back in the race and I ended up finishing second. Caitlin then went in and swam a great leg, before Becky swam the final leg and we won the bronze medal. It didn't really sink in what we had done straight afterwards. All I remember is thinking that we had done a good job. But when we went out to the podium in our tracksuits, the British swimming team was pool-side waiting for us 'doing an alley' – lining up to show they were thrilled with our success – and that moment was wonderful.

There were several highlights in 2010, the first at my home pool in Swansea as part of the GB team versus Germany, when I beat Rebecca Adlington and Jo Jackson, both Olympic medallists. The second was the Commonwealth Games in Delhi where I swam for Wales in the 200 and 400 metres freestyle races. I loved India and found everyone so friendly and welcoming to us. It was an amazing experience to be part of the Welsh team. In the 200 metres race I didn't put much pressure on myself as I didn't expect to do very well because I didn't have the front-end speed that some of the other girls had. So I wasn't as nervous as I normally am. I was in lane two, and I remember diving in and the girl in the next lane to me going off extremely fast. I remember thinking that I needed to stay in control, stay focussed and think about what I needed to do, rather than worry about her speed. My plan was to make sure that I used my 'back end' of race speed, so that in the last 50 metres I could come home fighting and, as I call it, get into sixth gear. I remember that at 150 metres, I was in sixth position. I turned for the fourth length and I fought so hard, kicking with everything I had to get into that final gear. I had to find something. It worked and I came away with the silver medal and a new Welsh record! It was the best feeling to see the Welsh team screaming for me in the stands! There were Welsh flags all around the pool. Unfortunately, my mum and dad couldn't come out to Delhi to support me but the flags were like having my whole family there. To gain a bronze medal in the 400 metres later made the Games outstanding for me: the first Welsh woman for decades to win two Commonwealth medals.

Being part of the Welsh team is a huge inspiration to me. The people of Swansea have sent wonderful messages of support to me, and the messages of congratulations I get through the Welsh team mean the world to me. It inspires me to try harder to make my country proud of me. Some of the texts, tweets and messages after the Commonwealth Games and the World Championships were so uplifting and, if I have a bad swim, they are the ones that I look at to make me feel good and motivate me again. Sport Wales and Swim Wales too have been fantastic to me. I am grateful for all their support. My coaches are inspirational and I appreciate all of the work they put in to help me give my best. My mum and dad too are amazing and I can't thank them enough for getting up at ridiculously early hours in the early days to take me to the pool for my training. I hope I can show them that all their efforts weren't for nothing and that my hard work is for them. Up until now I have combined swimming with my studies in Business Accounting and Finance at

Swansea University but next year I'm taking a year off to concentrate on the Olympics.

The countdown is on now for London 2012 and I am aiming to be part of the Olympic team competing in the fantastic new pool built especially for the Games. It's going to be such a great buzz with a crowd and the whole country getting behind the British team. Just to be part of it would be a dream come true. The trials are in March 2012 so I'll be training as hard as I can and doing everything in my power to ensure a place on that team.

Geraint Thomas

CYCLIST

Most people say I have an eye for talent ... Geraint has it in abundance, and with so many years to come the Welsh have a potential Classics and Grand Tour contender.

Shane Sutton OBE, GB Cycling Team Performance Manager

I've always loved cycling. I love the freedom, the chance to get out into the countryside on my bike and explore my surroundings. Being active and healthy is really important to me. Cycling is a great way to improve your fitness levels and, more than ever now, cycling is cool.

My dad bought me my first bike. It was a Giant, nothing special, but I loved it. A few years later he bought me a specialised bike which was a big step up, and to me this was amazing. I have great memories of my dad taking me to races on the weekends and travelling all over the country from Cardiff as far as Scotland. He was never pushy, never put any pressure on me, he was just there to help me. He always said that others were the race favourites so that I felt less nervous and knew they were the targets for me to take on. All he wanted for me was that I went out there and did my best. If I beat someone, his favourite expression was, 'That was a good scalp today!' He always talked about getting scalps and still uses that phrase with me today, when I beat a rival.

We weren't a cycling family. But my brother Alun and I started off together going to the Maindy Flyers cycling club in Cardiff at the age of ten and I really enjoyed the racing. In school I did the usual sports like rugby and athletics but I was always more interested in cycling because that's what I was best at. I started to win races and the prizes of fifty pounds were a lot of money to a kid. Above all, it was good fun and winning made it all the better. We raced every Thursday in a local mini league and I remember it being a great time, just going around on the track with my mates and having fun. My first coach, Debbie Wharton, saw me there and I remember her shouting, 'Can you go faster?' I started sprinting and knew this was it for me! It was what I wanted to do.

I got my first GB vest in 2000 for the British

Schools. I was selected the next year as well but this time they only sent out English vests rather than GB ones for us. But the important thing for me was to get into the competition and go out and race. Darren Tudor was the Welsh Junior coach and he took me on, and with him I won the Junior World Championship in 2004 and was second in the European Points race. I told him when he got a job with the British Cycling team that it was because of me and that he owed me ten per cent of his salary! I'm still waiting! (He's Head Coach with Welsh Cycling now, but I'm still claiming my fee!) I had competed in the World Junior Scratch race in Moscow the year before and came in around fifteenth but in the Championship in Los Angeles I was more confident and knew I could do well. I didn't expect to win, though. My family were there to support me and it was one of those dream days where everything came together and seemed easy. I won the sprint but I wasn't sure whether I had won the whole race or not. When they told me I had, I went crazy! It was my first big win and when you don't expect it, it's all the more sweet. Then, as we were lining up to go on the podium, the guy who was second told me that he had won and stood in ahead of me! I was confused, unsure what to do, when a judge appeared and confirmed that it was actually me who had won. Suddenly, it was believable, and I had the taste for winning. When I won the Paris–Roubaix Under-23 event, I was the first British rider ever to win it and everyone was excited for me because it proved I had a real future in the sport. In the same year, 2004, I won the Carwyn James Junior award at BBC Wales Sports Personality of the Year and I couldn't believe how good things were. I joined the British Olympic Academy for under 23-year-olds and moved to Manchester in preparation for great things ahead. I had to make a choice between joining the Academy or going to university – for me there was no contest.

But life doesn't always go to plan and my first real setback was in 2005, when I was training in Sydney. We were riding to the track on a big road into the city. There was a piece of corrugated iron on the ground and the rider in front of me hit it and his back wheel and my front wheel collided. It stopped me dead and I went down onto my handlebars. I wasn't bleeding and the skin wasn't punctured but the damage was internal. In the ambulance, the doctor asked me what I was doing in Australia and I answered, 'I'm racing in two days time.'

They looked shocked, but I was sure I would be all right. I just wanted to get back into training. At the hospital, the scan showed that I had ruptured my spleen and the doctor had to tell me that if I continued to bleed, I would die. He told me his concerns that if I crashed in the future it could rupture again. I wanted them to take it out straight away but he hesitated, saying that they would prefer to leave it in, if possible. But then the choice was made for them as it started bleeding again and they had to remove it. My mum and dad and my brother were flown out to Australia as the situation was serious. I was in intensive care and needed blood transfusions to get myself back on the road to recovery. But recover I did.

I won my first stage race in Luxembourg as a Senior in 2006. This was my first race back after having my spleen removed, so it was a huge boost for me. Also, I was following in the footsteps of Bradley Wiggins, and that made me proud. In 2007 I was the youngest rider in the Tour de France, and the first Welsh rider to compete in that great race since Colin Lewis in 1967. It was hard and I needed all of my strength, physical and mental, to survive. Every day I was 'on my knees' when I finished a stage. I would think to myself that there was no way I could start again the next day. I even sometimes thought, that's it, I'm going home. Then I'd wake up the next day and get on with it and I didn't want to stop once I started. The support of the crowds kept me going. It's great seeing Welsh flags when I'm riding in the Tour as I know they're there for me. The Tour de France is very special. The scale of the event is massive. Hordes of people come out to watch and to cheer, and the passion they have for the sport spurs you on. The media interest is intense and makes you realise how big an event it is around the world. I watched it in 1998 for the first time and I was immediately hooked. As a youngster I had taken part in the Kids Tour of Berlin over three days, with a stage every day. While I was doing it I'd thought that this must be what competing in the Tour de France was like! I dreamt of being there myself. When I eventually did take part, I had to pinch myself how far I had come from racing around the streets and imagining myself as a Tour de France rider. I was inspired by watching great riders and my heroes were very important to me.

One of my heroes was Welsh rider Nicole Cooke. Seeing her win competitions made it seem possible for me, as another Welsh rider, to do as well as she did. I really admire her determination and the way she gives it everything to get results. The way she rides is gutsy and strong, and her drive and ambition are clear. Bradley Wiggins is another important figure from the world of cycling, for the same reasons. Seeing Colin Jackson, another Welshman performing at the highest level, has also made me aspire to be better. Watching him compete in World Championships and Olympic Games put Wales on the map, and I wanted to do that, too.

Going to the Olympic Games in Beijing in 2008 didn't seem such a big deal at the time. We were in a holding camp in Newport, in our own little world, and really had no idea what was ahead of us. We flew out to China a week before the race and all of us were buzzing. The sprinters were doing well and everybody involved in cycling sensed something special. I had the opportunity of entering the individual pursuit but decided I wouldn't risk the team pursuit's chances, so kept myself for that race. The build-up was weird. Although we were in our own little world, you would see people around that you recognised and had seen on television, like Tyson Gay, the American sprinter, and Roger Federer, the Swiss tennis champion. The cycling team consisted of me, Paul Manning, Bradley Wiggins and Ed Clancy, who I shared a room with. We had been in the Under-23 Academy programme together and now to race with my best mate was fantastic. We were all very different personalities. Paul Manning was the oldest and he was the steady one. We call him Bern, after Bernard Manning the comedian, but he's nothing like that! Brad was very consistent and could be relied on to turn in regular fast times. As the youngsters, Ed and I would always blast it and then the two older guys would steady the ship and bring a bit of calm to the team. We must have done something right because we won the gold medal and broke the world record twice!

It didn't sink in for a while really, even though when we got back to Britain, it was all a big whirlwind. For days we were on open-top buses, involved in parades and got to meet the Queen. It wasn't until a few months later when I got home and saw the gold medal in the corner of the room, that I thought, yeah, that did actually happen! I also was awarded an MBE for that win. As a young boy, I'd grown up watching the Olympics with my father and brother and dreaming of being there myself, though not necessarily as a cyclist. Now I'd lived my dream.

48

Now everybody is talking about London 2012, but as cyclists it hasn't really hit us yet. We've got so many races before then that we haven't really thought about it. But after the Road Cycling World Championships which end the road season in September, and the start of the build-up at the European Track Cycling Championship in October, London will be the focus and will be in my mind the whole time. We train on the track twice a week in November and December, then all eyes will be on London.

Being so close to home, it will be very different. Beijing seemed a million miles away and only close friends and family could be there. It was so far away. This time, in London, it's going to be crazy!

Although cycling can be a very lonely pursuit, you rely on help and support to get to the top and stay there. You need hard work, commitment and talent and have to sacrifice a lot. I have to watch what I eat, rest properly and I can't go out on the town when I feel like it! We train for six hours a day sometimes and then go back to rest and recover before getting up the next day to do it all over again. I've probably spent less than a month in my house this year and I definitely miss my girlfriend Sara, and my mates. Just to do simple things like coming home to chill out, sitting on my own sofa and watching the TV is great. But I think I cope quite well with pressure. If you get to a race and you've done all the hard work and all the training, there's nothing more that you can do except get stuck in. Cycling has given me a great life. I've made great friends, visited so many countries and all the time doing something I love doing.

Things are going pretty well for me at the moment but you're only as good as your last race. It was great after this year's Tour de France that I was named as one of the ten guys that stood out from the tour. I am so grateful for all the help I have been given at Team Sky and particularly from Shane Sutton, the GB Cycling Team Performance Manager, who has been a huge influence on my career and Dan Hunt, my coach since the Olympics. The challenges to come are incredible. I just hope that I can make my family and Wales proud.

David Roberts

SWIMMER

David Roberts is a really inspirational athlete – to win 11 gold medals in any sport is phenomenal! It has been a privilege to be a part of his journey since Beijing, working with him at Definitive Sports Management and I look forward to seeing him winning more medals for Wales and Great Britain at his fourth Paralympic Games next year!

Jamie Baulch, Double World Champion – 400 metres and 4 × 400 metres

My dad was always the one in school who couldn't swim and he remembers being down in the shallow end, feeling left out, while the good swimmers had great fun in the deep end. He didn't want that ever to happen to his children. So at a very early age, I was taken by him to Abercynon Leisure Centre and he threw me in the water where his friend was waiting to catch me and give me my first swimming lesson.

They made swimming fun for me ... and the rest, as they say, is history!

Until the age of eleven, I was taken from doctor to doctor because I used to fall over a lot. I was always injuring myself and was taken regularly to hospital. I couldn't coordinate properly and my parents were told I was just a clumsy child. They were told not to mother me and to let me play like other boys. So I used to climb trees and play sport like other boys, but I used to get injured a lot more than them. Eventually, at the age of eleven, I went to see Dr John Morgan in the Occupational Therapy Department in East Glamorgan Hospital, and within ten minutes he had diagnosed cerebral palsy. So I went in a clumsy child and came out a disabled one. To me, though, it made no difference. I still wanted to play and climb and do all the other activities I was used to trying. Dr Morgan arranged physiotherapy for me with Dinah Cadogan who ran the Cardiff Wales Disabled Swimming club, and I have a great deal to thank Dr Morgan for, because he knew how to get the best for me. He understood the importance of being active and how it helped with my disability and, more importantly, what I could do to live life to the full. He understood the importance of finding physiotherapy that was fun and that you enjoyed and wanted to do.

When I was very young, I tried for my bronze ASA speed badge and, to the surprise of the teacher, I was quick enough to get the gold straight away. The teacher looked shocked and said that she had never seen anything like it, in twenty years of teaching! My mum and dad were really pleased and recognised that I had a talent, and were determined to help me as much as they could. I trained with Alan Iles who used to coach the Llantrisant Sharks and the Dragons Disabled Swimming Club. He was the first real influence on my swimming career and he became my personal coach until the Sydney Paralympics many years later. I remember all the work he put in to help me to achieve my potential. He was unlike any other coach I've known since, and had lots of different sayings to keep me motivated in the pool. One was to do 'floppy swimming' and I understood what that meant. I think for me it was a time to relax and enjoy myself, and he never put any pressure on me, I just had to go in and swim. I think as you get more professional, the sport becomes more structured and possibly a little less fun. But he made swimming fun for me, and it did the trick as he got me to my first Paralympic Games. I will always be grateful to him for that, and the gold medals that I won there in Sydney were for him, too. He was with me to enjoy the moment that he had helped to create. After I had swum, he just cried – it was so emotional for him. We'd decided what we needed to do, followed the plan and succeeded, he was very happy. For him his work was over. All he said was a quiet, 'Job done' but I could see how proud he was of me. That moment really was the beginning of all that I have been able to achieve in my swimming career this far.

My parents have never pushed me. They used to take me swimming as a form of physiotherapy and they've always allowed me to make my own decisions. I chose to be a swimmer and they supported my choice. My dad used to get up early, take me to my training session, sleep in his van while he waited for me to train, and then go to work, come home from work and take me training again. He did that every day of the week. I never had to ask him to do it, he was just my dad and that's what he did for me. My mum is probably the proudest mum you could ever meet but, like my dad, she's never pushed me either. She gets far more nervous than I ever do about my swimming and whatever the standard of competition, she is the one who worries.

At my school, Bryn Celynnog in Pontypridd, sport was very important. Many great Welsh athletes have come from this school – Neil Jenkins, Michael Owen, Kelly Morgan, Emma Brown and Sara Head. The school fostered sporting talent and really brought the best out in the students. Martin Sallan was my PE teacher and he knew that I would try everything. I tried to be in the school rugby team and the school football team, but it wasn't to be. But he'd always make sure my swimming talent was recognised. He and Elliot Williams, my Head of Year, promoted any successes I had and raised my confidence and self-esteem. Like Mr Lethbridge, my junior schoolteacher, they used my swimming success to inspire me. Being disabled, you can get bullied and great teachers who build you up are crucial. My attitude was always to stay positive and let my swimming do the talking. People did call me names but my swimming answered the bullies. I had a tight group of friends, too, and they made all the difference. Like many youngsters, I wanted to have a go in all kinds of sports, especially rugby, which I loved. I remember being devastated that

I wasn't allowed to play mini-rugby, as other parents were concerned that I would be hurt. I hated the idea that my disability would prevent me playing with the other boys. Eric Anthony, my wise and kindly rugby coach, finally had to take me aside and encourage me to concentrate on what I did best, my swimming. He knew that rugby would always be difficult for me, and chose to highlight and focus on what I could succeed in. I will always be grateful for his honesty, though I was shattered that I would never be picked for the Welsh rugby team!

However, in 1993 when I was thirteen, I was picked to swim for Wales. This was the greatest honour for a proud Welshman! I swam in the Rotary International in Glasgow against countries I'd never heard of and though I didn't win, I got the bug for competing. Five years later I was selected for Great Britain in the European Championships in Germany, where I gained four gold medals and broke four world records. Not a bad start! The first race was the 100 metres freestyle and I remember the thrill of being three seconds ahead at 50 metres and thinking how good it felt. I achieved a personal best and a world record. There is nothing better than the feeling of hitting the wall first and, with every win, my confidence increased. After that was the

4 × 100 metres freestyle relay. It was my first relay and I was joining a very experienced team. The others, Marc Woods, Jody Cundy and Matt Walker, were an established team of world champions and I learnt a lot as we smashed the world record. Sadly, my mum and dad weren't able to be there to see it, and my dad was actually more excited that he had seen a solar eclipse on the day I had won my medal – a different sort of gold for him that day! After that was the 50 metres freestyle where I beat the world champion and again broke the world record, and finally the 4 × 100 metres medley with the same result. It was a great feeling to know that all the hard work had paid off. Ahead were my first Paralympic Games and I was thrilled to be going.

What made the Sydney Paralympic Games even more special was that they were held in 2000, the millennium year. It was the first time my mum had been on an aeroplane and to have my family with me made it even more amazing. The opening ceremony was spectacular and seeing the Olympic flame being lit is a memory that will live with me forever. I couldn't believe that I, Dave Roberts from Beddau, was really there! I had to pinch myself to prove that I had really made it to the Paralympic Games. I went to see the pool beforehand and suddenly got a shiver as I realised just what I had come to do. The thought of racing in front of so many thousands was a sobering thought, especially in a country where swimming is the national sport! I thought back to the day that the letter inviting me to be part of the squad had arrived. My brother Rhys and I were jumping around the room ecstatic that all my dreams were coming true. When my kit arrived, I was like a kid in a sweet shop, pulling out all of the brand-new clothes from the two suitcases that had been sent. I was really proud of my blue tracksuit and all the other body suits and kit we had been given as part of the team.

Sport brings people from all countries together. It can be great fun as well as hard work. Some of the competitors I fear the most are great friends and the people I feel closest to. I met my girlfriend, Agata, through swimming and, for me, sport is also important in other areas of my life. We train hard and we play hard too! On our way to the opening ceremony, we went on a paddle-boat steamer to Darwin harbour for our team photo, and the atmosphere was electric. My mum and dad were in the crowd with an inflatable daffodil and Welsh flags. It's now a tradition and I know that I can always find them because of Dai the daffodil! He is marked up with all of the Games he's attended. I wasn't nervous. I was enjoying myself too much. I love the rush of excitement. I'm chilled out at competitions and happy and relaxed talking to people beforehand. For me, it's a day at work. I have a routine. I always look for Mum and Dad and wave. Then I put my goggles down on the block. Then I take my tracksuit off, and finally put the goggles on my head. Then I'm ready to go!

In Sydney, there were seven races and I brought home three gold medals, three silver medals and a bronze medal. For me, Sydney was huge fun but my medals showed how hard I had worked to get there. However, I did manage to climb a flagpole after competing as I wanted an Olympic flag to take home!

I remember my Paralympic Games through the music I listened to at the time. For Sydney it was the Manic Street Preachers. For Athens, it was the Beach Boys. Here, the medal tally was four golds and one silver medal, from six races. We didn't gain a medal in the relay but we did break the European record. In Beijing, the track I remember most was Kanye West's 'Stronger' and my medal tally was four gold medals in four races. Beijing was incredible in scale and size.

These were very different Games, much more ordered but equally exciting and powerful. My favourite swimming story in Beijing was that as part of the 4 × 100 metres freestyle relay team (with Graham Edmunds, Rob Welbourn and Matt Walker) we were told the Australians would beat us, even though we were going in as Olympic Champions. We had a plan! We decided to listen to our music through our headphones and go out in the order we would swim in, with our hoodies on and in a silent line. What we didn't know, because we had our hoodies up and our music on, was that the Star Wars theme was playing over the speakers in the pool. Apparently everyone thought we looked like Jedi warriors and it had rattled the Australians. We smashed the world record and our physiotherapist, Paul Martin, was thrilled because he had bet the Australian physiotherapist we would beat them and he'd been proved right! My eleventh gold was in the 50 metres freestyle against my closest rival, Matt Walker. He was confident, having beaten me in the trials, but, by 25 metres, I knew it was over and I had beaten him. I looked into the crowd where my coach Billy Pye was doing cartwheels in excitement. My mum, dad, my brother and my girlfriend Agata were in tears and I was proud of having done this for them, too. They were all so much a part of my success. Billy, my former coach, is someone I will always have ultimate respect for. Thanks to Billy, I've won eight gold medals and a silver. He gave me the confidence to do that. He gave me the training, the ability, the know-how and the strength. We were more like friends than coach and swimmer, and I saw him as a father figure to look up to. I was proud, too, of having equalled Dame Tanni Grey-Thompson's record. She was someone who I had always looked up to, a real Welsh hero.

I am very fortunate. To have been to one Paralympic Games is special but to have represented my country at three already is a huge honour. The Olympic day starts early at 5 am and eating is important! Meeting your coach and planning out the day ahead of you is crucial. I've always tried to win the heats to make sure I'm the fastest for the final and I always want the middle lane. Checking your kit, which you've checked six times already, becomes normal. I sleep and listen to music and, very importantly, listen to my coach. Then it's finally the moment. People react differently. I'm fairly relaxed and wave to my mum and dad. After the introductions to the crowd, the moment arrives and the race is on. Everyone asks how it feels when you win – it's brilliant! You shake hands with your rivals, you talk to the press and enjoy the medal presentation. After that, you always check your bag to make sure your medal is safe and when you arrive back at the village and go into the food hall, someone starts clapping. During that night, you check your medal at least a hundred times and then sleep with it!

The Paralympics have meant everything to me. For my services to disabled sport in the Paralympics, I was awarded the CBE. London 2012 will be my last. I need now to remain injury- and accident-free to be fully fit as I go for my twelfth gold medal. It is a huge challenge but the prospect of not competing is unthinkable, despite a recent spate of bad luck and freak accidents. I've just got to be there in London – if I wasn't, I'd never forgive myself. I'm nervous about the future after that but there will be other challenges and opportunities to come. I go into London 2012 with a strong and supportive team around me. It includes Jamie Baulch, an Olympic athlete in his own right and trusted friend and agent, with Peter Key as my coach – I am the first disabled swimmer in his top squad. In addition, Jaguar and Lloyds TSB have provided much-needed practical support. Team Roberts is ready and looking forward to be part of London 2012 and to be there competing in home Games. From Sydney to Stratford, it's been quite a journey!

Quick Reads📖
Books in the Quick Reads series

Quick Reads 📖

Fall in love with reading

Earnie: My Life with Cardiff City
Robert Earnshaw

Accent Press

From the African plains to the Millennium Stadium, this is the remarkable story of the boy who was born to be a Bluebird.

Nicknamed Earnie, this is the story of Robert Earnshaw's journey from the Zambian village where he was born to Caerphilly, where he first kicked a 'proper' football. Seven years later, aged 16, he was signed up by Cardiff City and started banging in the goals on his way to break the Bluebirds' goal-scoring records.

Here Earnie reflects on his Welsh success, his trademark somersault goal celebration and the crazy world of Sam Hammam, and he reveals why Cardiff City will always have a special place in his heart.

Quick Reads 📖

Fall in love with reading

Why do Golf Balls have Dimples?
Wendy Sadler

Accent Press

Have you ever wondered why golf balls have dimples or why your hair goes frizzy in the rain?
   Scientist Wendy Sadler has the answers in her book of Weird and Wonderful facts.

Broken down into user-friendly chapters like sport, going out, the great outdoors, food and drink and the downright weird, Wendy's book gives the scientific answers to life's intriguing questions, like why toast always lands butter-side down and why you can't get (too) lost with a satnav.